U.S. Department of Justice
Office of Justice Programs
Office of Juvenile Justice and Delinquency Prevention

J. Robert Flores, Administrator | Juvenile Justice Practices Series

JUVENILE JUSTICE BULLETIN

August 2005

Planning Community-Based Facilities for Violent Juvenile Offenders as Part of a System of Graduated Sanctions

Shelley Zavlek

The Office of Juvenile Justice and Delinquency Prevention (OJJDP) is presenting a Juvenile Justice Practices Series to provide the field with updated research, promising practices, and tools for a variety of juvenile justice areas. These Bulletins are important resources for youth-serving professionals involved in developing and adopting juvenile justice policies and programs, regardless of their funding sources.

This fourth Bulletin in the series discusses the use of small, secure, community-based or regional facilities to house serious, violent, and/or chronic juvenile offenders.[1]

In the early 1990s, the prevailing belief was that serious juvenile crime was out of control and bound to get worse. These projections, although credible at the time, failed to materialize. On the contrary, serious juvenile crime rates have been declining over the past decade and, as of 2001, were at their lowest level since 1983 (Snyder, 2003). Nevertheless, the rate at which youth have been placed in confinement in the United States nearly doubled between 1979 and 2001 (Hobbs and Nicole, 2002; Snyder and Sickmund, 1999; Sickmund, 2002; Sickmund, Sladky, and Kang, 2004). The causes of these apparently contradictory trends are complex, and the end result is troubling: most youth housed in today's large, secure juvenile facilities do not require the level of security these facilities were created to provide. Furthermore, research suggests that simply "locking kids up" in such facilities is an ineffective and unnecessarily expensive approach to helping troubled youth and reducing juvenile crime. Jurisdictions are seeking better strategies.

---

[1] OJJDP first focused attention on treatment and intervention strategies for this population of juvenile offenders in its *Comprehensive Strategy for Serious, Violent, and Chronic Juvenile Offenders* (Wilson and Howell, 1993). This group includes juveniles who commit serious violent and nonviolent offenses and juveniles who have had multiple contacts with the justice system. Loeber and Farrington define "serious violent offenses" as homicide, rape, robbery, aggravated assault, and kidnapping and "serious nonviolent offenses" as burglary, motor vehicle theft, theft over $100, arson, and drug trafficking (Loeber and Farrington, 1998, p. xix). "Chronic offenders" are defined as those who have had five or more police contacts (Wilson and Howell, 1993, p. 2).

A promising strategy for responding to juvenile crime is one in which secure confinement is an integral part of a continuum of options that also includes prevention, comprehensive services, graduated sanctions, and, for confined youth, aftercare programming to ensure successful reentry into the community. For each youth who comes to the attention of the juvenile justice system, the best response is the least restrictive one that meets the needs of the youth and the community. Secure confinement is reserved for the small number of offenders who pose a threat to public safety, account for a disproportionate share of all serious crime committed by juveniles, and are unsuitable for other settings or programs.

For this limited population of serious, violent, and/or chronic juvenile offenders, smaller, community-based or regional facilities can provide secure confinement economically and with the best possible outcomes for the youth involved. This Bulletin presents basic information relevant to planning such facilities. After a brief review of juvenile arrest and incarceration trends, the Bulletin discusses the advantages of small, secure, community-based or regional facilities and outlines a process for developing such facilities within a comprehensive juvenile justice system master plan. The Bulletin also describes three sample programs and presents a list of related resources.

Background

The mid-1980s and early 1990s saw a precipitous rise in violent juvenile crime, a projected surge in the juvenile population, and sporadic, high-profile incidents of youth crime, such as the shootings at schools in Jonesboro, AK, and Paducah, KY, and at Columbine High School in Littleton, CO. In the early 1990s, warnings of an emerging class of "violent juvenile superpredators" aroused public fears. In a 1996 report by the Coordinating Council on Juvenile Justice and Delinquency Prevention, U.S. Attorney General Janet Reno stated that "[n]o corner of America is safe from increasing levels of criminal violence, including violence committed by and against juveniles" (p. iii). The report issued an urgent call to action:

> This Nation must take immediate and decisive action to intervene in the problem of juvenile violence that threatens the safety and security of communities—and the future of our children—across the country. Demographic experts predict that juvenile arrests for violent crimes will more than double by the year 2010, given population growth projections and trends in juvenile arrests over the past several decades (p. 1).

Reports of uncontrolled juvenile crime fueled fears that America was under assault by a generation of "teenage time bombs" and that "only the abandonment of 'soft' educational and rehabilitative approaches, in favor of strict and unrelenting discipline—a zero tolerance approach" could address the problem (Browne, 2003, p. 10).

By the mid-1990s, however, the overall juvenile arrest rate for violent offenses—murder, rape, robbery, and aggravated assault—was as low as it had been a generation earlier, and the rate has since declined even further. In 2002 (the most recent year for which data are available), the rate was nearly half its 1994 peak level. Between 1993 and 2002, the juvenile arrest rate for murder dropped 64 percent, rape 27 percent, robbery 38 percent, and assault 34 percent. In addition, the juvenile arrest rate for property crimes dropped 34 percent between 1993 and 2002 (Snyder, 2004).

Nevertheless, during the 1990s, legislators reacting to real and perceived public concerns determined to "crack down" on juvenile crime (McCord, Widom, and Crowell, 2001). Nationwide, states and local jurisdictions enacted new laws that imposed tougher sanctions on juvenile offenders—more mandatory and determinate sentences, blended sentencing (combining juvenile and adult sanctions), more offenses that qualified for the most severe sentences, progressive sanctions, and "zero tolerance" policies (Browne, 2003; Torbet et al., 1996; Torbet and Szymanski, 1998; Howell, 1997). These legislative reforms, together with juvenile justice system policy changes, brought more youth into the system for longer periods of time. In addition, the system experienced an influx of youth with severe emotional, behavioral, and mental health problems (Teplin et al., 2002; Parent et al., 1994).

Thus, although serious juvenile crime rates in 2001 were comparable to rates 20 years earlier, the number of youth confined in juvenile residential facilities on any given day nearly doubled during the same period of time. In fact, whereas the total population of youth ages 10–19 increased only slightly more than 3 percent between 1980 and 2000,[2] the number of juveniles confined on an average day rose from 51,000 in 1979 to more than 104,000 in 2001—an increase of more than 100 percent (Snyder and Sickmund, 1999; Sickmund, 2002; Sickmund, Sladky, and Kang, 2004). As noted earlier, the juvenile violent crime arrest rate rose sharply during the mid-1980s and early 1990s, from 139 arrests per 100,000 youth ages 17 and younger in 1985 to 231 arrests per 100,000 youth in 1994—a 66-percent increase. However, as noted in a report by the Annie E. Casey Foundation (Stanfield, 1999), the number of youth confined in detention centers on an average day increased even more—74 percent—during approximately the same period of time (from 1985 to 1995). Moreover, although the juvenile violent crime arrest rate has declined dramatically since 1994—more than 44 percent from 1994 to 2001—there has not been a concomitant decline in juvenile confinement, which has remained fairly constant since 1995 (Snyder, 2003).

The increased reliance on confinement placed a large burden on existing juvenile detention and correctional facilities, many of which were reaching the end of their useful lives by the mid-1990s. Between 1991 and 1995, the number of youth committed to overcapacity training schools and long-term public institutions (i.e., facilities with more residents than they were designed to house) increased 55 percent. By 1995, nearly 70 percent of youth confined in public juvenile facilities were held in overcapacity facilities (Snyder and Sickmund, 1999). Furthermore, facilities built in the 1960s and 1970s were designed primarily for youth charged with petty crimes and status offenses, such as shoplifting and truancy. Few facilities were prepared to provide treatment and services for the more challenging populations placed in their custody during the 1980s and 1990s (Teplin et al., 2002; Roush and McMillen, 2000; Cocozza, 1992).

In the mid-1990s, studies such as *Conditions of Confinement: Juvenile Detention and Corrections Facilities* (Parent et al., 1994) and *Beyond the Walls: Improving the Conditions of Confinement for Youth in Custody* (Puritz and Scali, 1998) documented widespread overcrowding and substandard, dangerous conditions in juvenile facilities. The need to replace or renovate these facilities became apparent, and funds were allocated accordingly.

The need to add space to address existing safety and overcrowding conditions does not fully explain the increase in youth detention facility construction. Nor does it explain the development and construction of large facilities as opposed to smaller ones. Many juvenile systems and jurisdictions have developed larger facilities, containing anywhere from 150 to more than 800 juvenile beds.[3] Such facilities, with their physically restrictive construction and sophisticated security and communications systems, are among the most expensive structures that public agencies build and are extraordinarily expensive to operate (Griffinger, 2001). A 1998 report on crowding in detention facilities recognized secure detention as "by far, the most expensive option for handling youth undergoing juvenile delinquency proceedings" (Burrell et al., 1998, p. 12). The extraordinary costs the report cites for secure facilities include both operating and construction costs. Based on a 2000 report, total juvenile justice expenditures in the United States are at

---

[2] According to U.S. Census data, the total U.S. population ages 10–19 increased 3.39 percent between 1980 and 2000 (Hobbs and Nicole, 2002).

[3] For example, the 865-bed Chaderjian Youth Correctional Facility in Stockton, CA, opened in 1991; the 450-bed Michigan Youth Correctional Facility opened in 1999; and in Texas, the 436-bed Orientation and Assessment Unit opened in Marlin in 1995, the 356-bed San Saha State School opened in 1996, the 336-bed Victory Field Correctional Academy opened in 1997, and the 352-bed McLennan County State Juvenile Correctional Facility opened in 2000 (American Correctional Association, 2001).

least $10–15 billion, with much of that amount paying for confinement of a small segment of the juvenile offender population, most of whom are housed in training schools or "large correctional units typically housing 100 to 500 youth" (Mendel, 2000, p. 49).

Today, many of the youth housed in juvenile correctional facilities pose little threat to the community. A 1993 study of incarcerated juveniles in 14 states revealed that violent offenders comprised a minority of youth in confinement, ranging from a high of 44 percent to a low of 11 percent (Krisberg et al., 1993). The 2001 Census of Juveniles in Residential Placement (CJRP) found that of the 76,298 youth residing in juvenile facilities as a result of court-ordered placements, 18,321—24 percent—had committed a Violent Crime Index offense (homicide, sexual assault, robbery, or aggravated assault). According to the CJRP, 23 percent of all youth in court-ordered placements had committed a combination of technical violations, status offenses, and other public order offenses (excluding weapons).[4] A similar pattern was evident with youth held in temporary detention centers while awaiting trial (Sickmund, Sladky, and Kang, 2004). In addition, many youth are incarcerated simply because of a shortage of alternatives—in particular, community-based services and mental health services—that might prevent them from entering the juvenile justice system (Griffinger, 2001; Stanfield, 1999).

Youth in juvenile correctional facilities may be subjected to harsh conditions. In its assessment of juvenile facilities, the National Research Council Panel on Juvenile Crime concluded that

> [d]etained and incarcerated juveniles have higher rates of physical injury, mental health problems, and suicide attempts and have poorer educational outcomes than do their counterparts who are treated in the community. Detention and incarceration also cause severe and long-term problems with future employment, leaving ex-offenders with few economic alternatives to crime. (McCord, Widom, and Crowell, 2001, p. 223)

Furthermore, a large, centralized facility unavoidably removes most youth from their community environments and local cultures.[5] This increases alienation and isolates youth exclusively with other delinquent peers, which "tends to exacerbate rather than mitigate the law-breaking tendencies of youthful offenders" (Mendel, 2000, p. 49; Krisberg and Howell, 1998).

Serious, pervasive problems in the juvenile justice system—such as inadequate risk assessment procedures, lack of alternative programs, inadequate special programs (e.g., mental health, gender-specific), and poor supervision in probation and aftercare—all contribute to overcrowding in juvenile correctional facilities, which further adds to the harshness of conditions in these facilities. The lack or inadequacy of diversionary tools results in increased use of secure facilities as a catch-all solution (Mendel, 2001; Burrell et al., 1998).

The foregoing factors all underline the need for jurisdictions to examine carefully their approach to using secure confinement. To ensure that public funds are spent wisely, civic authorities responsible for juvenile justice planning must pursue a full range of custodial and service options to both protect the public and provide an appropriate, fiscally prudent response to juvenile treatment and supervision needs. Simply continuing to add secure bedspace will not suffice. The key is better designed programs and facilities that

---

[4] Technical violations include violation of probation, parole, valid court orders, or conditions of probation or parole. Status offenses include obstruction of justice, nonviolent sex offenses, cruelty to animals, disorderly conduct, traffic offenses, etc.

[5] On January 31, 2005, the California Youth Authority (CYA) announced the terms of a settlement reached in a lawsuit concerning conditions of confinement in the juvenile justice system. The settlement stated that in conjunction with developing a wholly new model for juvenile corrections in California, CYA would keep youth in facilities close to their homes.

address emerging needs. Jurisdictions must conduct the necessary research and engage in comprehensive planning processes to reach sound decisions regarding the need for secure beds for juveniles (Roush and McMillen, 2000; Zavlek and Barron, 2000). The remaining sections of this Bulletin address these tasks.

Advantages of Small, Community-Based Secure Facilities

Serious, violent, and chronic juvenile offenders may require placement in secure facilities to protect the public, hold the offenders accountable for their acts, and provide an appropriate treatment environment. Although training schools, camps, and ranches may still have some limited use for these purposes, most authorities agree that such "large congregate-care juvenile facilities . . . have not proven to be particularly effective in rehabilitating juvenile offenders" (Krisberg and Howell, 1998, p. 362).

The most effective strategy for treating and rehabilitating juvenile offenders and preventing recidivism is a comprehensive, community-based model that integrates prevention programming; a continuum of pretrial and sentencing placement options, services, and sanctions; and aftercare programs (Loeber and Farrington, 1998; Howell, 1995; Altschuler and Armstrong, 1994). This model reserves secure placement for only the most violent and serious juvenile offenders (Loeber and Farrington, 1998)—those who cannot function in a less restrictive environment or who pose a threat to public safety. Leading authorities point to the advantages of small, community-based facilities for housing the relatively few juvenile offenders who require a secure, structured setting (Krisberg and Howell, 1998). Even for jurisdictions under pressure to "get tough" on juvenile crime, planning new facilities within this framework has programmatic, economic, and systemwide advantages.

Programmatic Advantages

Decentralizing facilities for juvenile offenders has programmatic advantages that benefit juvenile justice systems, youth and families that come in contact with these systems, and communities as a whole. These advantages derive from (1) keeping young offenders connected to their communities and (2) targeting sanctions and services to meet the needs of specific jurisdictions and categories of offenders.

Research indicates that many incarcerated youth can be managed effectively in well-structured, community-based programs. Krisberg and Howell (1998) summarize the results of some of the most frequently referenced studies on alternatives to institutionalization for serious juvenile offenders. Most of these studies found greater or similar reductions in recidivism rates and greater attitudinal improvements in youth treated in community-based programs as compared to those placed in secure institutions. These studies led researchers to suspect that "alternatives to secure confinement for serious and chronic juveniles are at least as effective in suppressing recidivism as incarceration, but are considerably less costly to operate" (Krisberg and Howell, 1998, p. 360). When secure confinement is necessary, "the establishment of small, community-based facilities to provide intensive services in a secure environment offers the best hope for successful treatment of those juveniles who require a structured setting" (Krisberg and Howell, 1998, p. 362).

Based on this research, states considering new facilities have an opportunity to replace large, traditional training schools with smaller, community-based or regional facilities that are part of a continuum of services and sanctions supported by local justice systems and communities (Austin, Johnson, and Weitzer, forthcoming). Such facilities are more likely to be rooted in local values, engender community support and involvement, and reflect the needs of local jurisdictions. Equally important, these smaller facilities can target programming and operations to be responsive to the specific treatment and supervision needs of the youth in their care. By focusing exclusively on serious, violent, and/or chronic juvenile offenders, these facilities can avoid the operational problems that arise when disparate behavioral groups are housed together.

Developing small, secure, community-based or regional facilities to hold serious, violent, and/or chronic juvenile offenders who are identified as unsuitable for other settings or programs also creates a valuable opportunity to address the most serious problems of youth crime and recidivism. This relatively small group of offenders accounts for a disproportionate share of all serious crime committed by juveniles (Loeber and Farrington, 1998). Furthermore, studies have shown substantial recidivism among juveniles released from residential institutions.[6] Clearly, just locking up these youth is not enough. It is critically important to provide effective treatment programs designed to enhance their chances for success when they return to the community. A smaller residential facility that houses only the most serious offenders can be an ideal setting for such programs.

Although few studies have examined the impact of criminal sanctions on juvenile crime rates, some research indicates that effective programming for serious and violent offenders can produce modest to substantial reductions in recidivism rates. A meta-analysis involving 200 studies that investigated the effects of interventions with serious juvenile offenders (83 of which dealt with programs for institutionalized youth) found that "for both institutionalized and noninstitutionalized offenders, the 'average' intervention program represented in the research literature produced positive, statistically significant effects equivalent to about a 12% reduction in subsequent reoffense rates" (Lipsey and Wilson, 1998, p. 338). However, the most effective treatment programs for institutionalized juveniles, which focused on interpersonal skills (e.g., social skills training, anger management, and moral education) and used behavioral programs (e.g., cognitive mediation training, stress inoculation training, reinforcement therapy principles), reduced recidivism rates by as much as 40 percent (Lipsey and Wilson, 1998). These and other researchers have concluded that developing successful facilities and treatment models for serious, violent, and/or chronic juvenile offenders is programmatically sound and makes both intuitive and fiscal sense considering the expense and social costs associated with the delinquent behavior of these juvenile offenders (Lipsey and Wilson, 1998; Wiebush et al., 1995; Altschuler, 1998).

Smaller facilities connected to local communities have programmatic advantages that are generally missing from large congregate-care facilities, which often confine youth hundreds of miles from their families and the communities they will reenter when they are released. Small, community-based or regional facilities can:

♦ Engage local communities to provide resources for creating a comprehensive prevention, sanction, and treatment model. Potential community partners include service providers, volunteers and mentors, houses of worship, schools, civic organizations, businesses, and government agencies.

♦ Help youth forge personal bonds with mentors and other caring adults in the community. A key factor for healthy development is the "capacity, ability, and opportunity to build relationships with caring adults" (Masten and Coatsworth, 1998). Studies of successful youth who live in high-risk environments indicate the critical importance of strong bonds with caregivers or other adults in preventing problem behaviors (Hawkins, Catalano, and Miller, 1992).

♦ Engage in ongoing, intensive family involvement and intervention activities. This approach recognizes the critical role of families in treating young offenders (Thornberry, 1993).

♦ Function as a resource for the community (e.g., through victim counseling and restitution programs).

A facility that is located in the community can also offer youth enhanced opportunities for independent living. Administrators can create phased reentry programs that allow youth and their support networks to participate in a gradual and successful transition back into the community.

---

[6] A recent study of recidivism among incarcerated offenders in 15 states found that 82 percent of juveniles ages 14–17 were rearrested within 3 years of their release; among those serving time for violent offenses, the rate was 62 percent (Langan and Levin, 2002). A number of state studies confirm high recidivism rates (more than 50 percent) among juvenile offenders released from confinement (Feld, 1998; Howell, 1997).

Economic Advantages

A more localized system of sanctions and services for juvenile offenders has economic as well as programmatic advantages. Jurisdictions that adopt this strategy can expect cost savings in three areas: facility operations, recidivism, and facility construction.

Downsizing large, centralized facilities—i.e., replacing them with a system of smaller, community-based or regional facilities that are part of a full continuum of sanctions and services—is likely to produce substantial immediate and long-term savings in the form of lower operating costs and reduced recidivism (Loeber and Farrington, 1998). Secure facilities are particularly expensive to operate because they run 24 hours a day, 365 days a year, and have relatively high staffing ratios. Reforms that emphasize using the least restrictive sanction consistent with the needs of offenders and the safety of the community will result in reduced operating costs as many youth are moved out of secure confinement and into less expensive alternatives. In addition, reduced recidivism is likely to result as both secure facilities and other sanctions and services are better tailored to the needs of the juveniles and jurisdictions they serve.

Construction costs are an additional consideration. High-security facilities are the most expensive to construct. Costs associated with building materials, security systems, furniture, fixtures, and equipment for these facilities far exceed the costs of standard commercial-grade items that can be used in other facilities. If a jurisdiction decides it does not need to build a high-security facility and can instead substitute a lower security facility or a nonresidential program, cost savings will result.

Because secure facilities are expensive to build and operate, it is important for jurisdictions to recognize when secure incarceration is being used inappropriately for youth who can be successfully treated in other settings. Although more rigorous research into appropriate sanctions for the most serious juvenile offenders may be needed, leading authorities recognize that "community-based interventions for serious and chronic offenders can be safely expanded, and produce enormous cost savings" (Krisberg and Howell, 1998).

Systemwide Advantages

Creating a new small, secure, community-based facility (or a small, secure regional facility in less populated areas) offers an opportunity to improve the entire continuum of services and sanctions for at-risk and delinquent youth in the community. In developing such a facility, it is critical to understand that the facility should not stand alone but rather should be designed as an integrated part of this continuum. For example, by providing space and access for community-based service providers, the facility design can make it possible for these providers to begin working with youth while they are still in custody, thus ensuring continuity of services and helping the facility tap into the strengths and resources of the community.

Many jurisdictions are developing juvenile justice facilities that incorporate multiple aspects of the local continuum of services into the facility design. This approach achieves economies of scale by allowing various smaller programs and facilities to be housed either in a single multiservice center or in a campus-style setting. Furthermore, construction and operating expenses can be shared among several cost centers.

Although such facilities can offer clear advantages for a community, extensive teamwork and planning should precede the decision to build them.[7] Juvenile justice system stakeholders need to work together toward a common goal: a system of facilities and programs that holds young offenders accountable

---

[7] Jurisdictions should take caution to control the total bed capacity of a multiservice facility, keeping each residential component (detention, secure treatment, group home, etc.) relatively small—no larger than about 50 beds. The total capacity should reflect careful analysis of the juvenile offender population and related bedspace needs.

through a continuum of graduated sanctions while building strengths and resilience in these youth through a broad spectrum of services such as education, mental health, skills training, and intensive aftercare supervision.[8]

Missouri: A Case Study in Cost-Effective Reforms

In 1983, Missouri closed its only large training school and moved to a well-developed system of regional, small-scale correctional centers and community-based residential and nonresidential programs. The state also moved from an incarceration model to a rehabilitation model. In 1994, Missouri appropriated funds to construct 200 secure beds, with the condition that no facility could exceed a 50-bed capacity. By 2001, no juvenile correctional facility in Missouri contained more than 85 beds, and all except 3 contained 33 beds or fewer.[a] Missouri also created an objective decisionmaking strategy to provide juvenile justice professionals with standardized procedures for screening, assessing, and assigning dispositions to juvenile offenders (Hsia and Beyer, 2000).

As a result of these reforms, three-fourths of youthful offenders committed to Missouri's Division of Youth Services (DYS) are assigned to nonresidential community programs, group homes, and less secure residential facilities. Youth who are committed to the state's medium- and high-security facilities enter a bright, noninstitutional environment that provides extensive, 24-hour-per-day therapy, quality education programs, strong family outreach and counseling, well-qualified and highly trained staff, and extensive aftercare support (Mendel, 2001).

A report sponsored by The American Youth Policy Forum concluded that Missouri's focus on treatment and use of least restrictive care rather than incarceration and punishment "is far more successful and cost-effective than the training school-oriented systems of most state juvenile corrections agencies" (Mendel, 2001, p. 11). Cost savings have resulted from avoiding overreliance on expensive residential confinement programs, limiting length of stay in residential programs, and reducing recidivism. Reported recidivism rates have declined from 50 percent or more in the old training school model to averages as low as 11 percent (Center on Juvenile & Criminal Justice, 2004). According to state records, currently only 8 percent of youth released from rehabilitative programs are in Missouri's prisons 5 years after their release. Based on regional per diem costs for secure confinement of juveniles, Missouri's reduced reliance on incarceration saves $140 per day ($51,000 per year) for each bed not used (because of reduced recidivism, use of alternatives, and other reforms). In addition, as a result of Missouri's reforms, DYS operated in 2000 with a budget of $61 million (about $94 per youth in the state's population ages 10–17); the average juvenile corrections budget in the eight states surrounding Missouri was approximately $140 per youth—one-third more than Missouri's budget (Mendel, 2001).

Representatives from several states have visited Missouri to learn more about its reforms, and many are beginning to follow Missouri's lead.[b] On January 31, 2005, as part of the settlement of a lawsuit challenging conditions in the California Youth Authority (CYA), CYA announced a plan to completely reform California's juvenile justice system based largely on Missouri's rehabilitative model and therapeutic environments. CYA's new model will include families in treatment and rehabilitation, keep youth in facilities close to their homes, provide youth with a supportive and positive environment that helps them get their lives back on track, and staff programs with trained rehabilitation specialists.

---

[a] The Fulton Treatment Center, described under "Sample Programs," was the prototype for these smaller facilities.
[b] Author's interviews with DYS Director Mark Steward.

---

[8] These services have been identified as essential to the successful reintegration of young offenders into their communities (Altschuler and Armstrong, 1994).

The stakeholder team's first challenge is to establish links among all components of the existing system of services and sanctions, including prevention, diversion, probation, nonsecure sanctioning alternatives, secure sanctions, and aftercare. Once the links are established, the team should analyze the populations entering the juvenile justice system, ensure that alternatives to incarceration are used effectively, and develop new secure confinement facilities only when warranted. The links established by the stakeholder team are also essential for implementing effective case management and family involvement procedures at each stage of the juvenile justice process, from entry into the system through release.

The next two sections elaborate on this planning process. They discuss both the context and the "nuts and bolts" of facility planning.

> **The Multiservice Facility: An Example From Eugene, OR**
>
> The Lane County Juvenile Justice Center in Eugene, OR, is a secure, co-ed, 36-bed facility that houses the county's Department of Youth Services (intake, probation, parole, and detention center); juvenile court, court clerk, district attorneys, and defense attorneys; Court Appointed Special Advocates (CASA); and the Oregon Youth Authority. The facility, which houses both preadjudicated and postadjudicated youth, also offers a drug and alcohol treatment program, assessments, and shelter care.

A Systemic Approach to Facility Planning

A comprehensive juvenile justice system master plan is a prerequisite for developing new facilities and programs to ensure an appropriate continuum of residential and nonresidential services. "Master planning" means that juvenile justice agencies and civic authorities should:

♦ Know the populations their system serves.

♦ Select the best approaches for meeting the needs of youth and the community, based on clearly defined values and goals.

♦ Actively plan for all essential services and programs, addressing issues such as funding, staffing, and space needs.

The starting point for this process is a thorough assessment of the juvenile justice system. That requires the participation of all stakeholders in the system.

Participatory Planning: Building Consensus Among Stakeholders

The process of system assessment should be fully participatory. To achieve full participation, a steering committee consisting of key stakeholders should be established, including representatives from every level of government, probation and community corrections, existing facilities, social services, the judiciary, prosecuting attorneys, schools, child advocates, parents, and business leaders. Steering committee members should be individuals who:

♦ Understand the local community.

♦ Possess the necessary knowledge and skills to tailor a system plan and programs to local needs.

♦ Know how to get things done in the community.

♦ Have the power to implement the selected sentencing sanctions, programs, and plans broadly and to monitor their effects to make adjustments as needed. (Catalano et al., 1998)

Stakeholders may have very different and sometimes competing goals and interests. They may also have very different views about the objectives of the juvenile justice system and about critical decisions that affect juveniles at various points in the system (figure 1).

Figure 1. Key Decision Points in the Juvenile Justice System: Illustrative System Objectives and Decision Options

Arrest

Arrest/ Referral	Intake/ Detention

System objectives:
- Conduct initial assessment
- De-escalate and stabilize
- Refer accused for formal adjudication
- Prevent further offending
- Assure initial court appearance

Decision options:
- Warn and release
- Issue citation or summons
- Refer to law enforcement diversion
- Refer to services
- Take youth into custody
  -- Conduct intake and assessment
  -- Provide crisis services
  -- Detain pending court hearing
  -- Release with or without conditions pending court hearing

Adjudication

Case Filing	Pretrial Release or Detention	Trial/ Adjudication	Sentencing/ Disposition

System objectives:
- Determine need for formal adjudication
- Determine guilt or innocence
- Evaluate the situation of the accused and his or her amenability to intervention
- Maintain the accused and prevent further offending during case processing

Decision options:
- File petition or divert from formal adjudication
- Determine need for continued detention during adjudication
- If eligible for release pending adjudication, set release conditions
- Refer to services (voluntary or as a condition of release)

Decision options:
- Determine guilt or innocence
- Determine need for pre-disposition evaluation
- Determine disposition
  -- No intervention
  -- Civil fine or penalty
  -- Probation with or without conditions
  -- Commitment to state custody

Disposition

Sanction/Sentence Modification

System objectives:
- Protect the community
- Hold offenders accountable
- Rehabilitate
- Prevent future crime

Decision options:
- Placement (ranging from home to secure setting)
- Supervision level
- Services required
- Progress in meeting court orders or case plan goals
- Revocation if court ordered conditions not met
- Discharge

Postdisposition

Aftercare

System objectives:
- Support successful reintegration into the community
- Rehabilitate
- Prevent future crime

Decision options:
- Reentry services required
  -- Placement
  -- Level of supervision
  -- Services required
- Progress in meeting aftercare goals
- Revocation if release conditions not met
- Discharge

Source: S. Zavlek, IPFYouth

Steering committee members should reach a consensus regarding objectives and decisionmaking criteria for each phase of the juvenile justice caseflow process. Consensus is achieved through structured workshops that encourage an open exchange of ideas. These workshops usually move from the general (agreeing on broad values, creating vision and mission statements) to the very specific (spelling out goals and objectives). (A similar process takes place in developing a facility master plan, as discussed in greater detail below.)

Consensus building is important because decisions in the caseflow process are governed as much by policy as by the behavior of juveniles. Policy changes can have a dramatic impact on costs and system outcomes. Careful assessment and planning can ensure that the juvenile justice system is responsive to the needs of youth and the community. For these reasons, it is essential that all stakeholders and other interested parties remain fully engaged throughout the assessment and planning process.

Juvenile Justice System Assessment

A juvenile justice system assessment is a collaborative information-gathering and analysis process conducted to gain a better understanding of how an existing system of sanctions and services works; to identify any duplication, gaps, needs, and excesses; and to determine where a proposed new facility would fit within the system (figure 2). The assessment should result in detailed baseline data and analyses that can be used to develop a more coordinated, rational, and cost-effective system.

The assessment should consider all factors that affect demands on and use of sanctions and services. It should also examine all factors that drive the need for new detention and corrections beds, including the following: (1) policies, practices, and available resources; (2) arrest rates for various types of crimes; (3) speed with which the justice system processes cases; and (4) availability and use of alternatives to secure confinement.

Steps in the juvenile justice system assessment process include developing profiles of the community and the existing juvenile justice system, assessing other community resources, developing baseline information about how the sanctioning system currently operates, and researching historical justice system trends and analyzing data. The box that follows figure 2 outlines details of these steps.

Completing a system assessment requires many meetings. Participants include steering committee and assessment team members, public officials and policymakers, community leaders and citizens, and juvenile justice decisionmakers. The goal of the meetings is a consensus about the current status of the juvenile justice system, how well it is working, and how it might be improved.

Assessment results may be used to reevaluate or modify available sanctioning options, programs, and processes; refine forecasts of future bedspace needs; and identify opportunities for improving management of existing bedspace capacity. Information from the assessment provides a basis for shaping a vision of how the system might look in the future and for developing a strategy to realize that vision.

Figure 2. Key Decision Points in the Juvenile Justice System: Illustrative Intervention Options and Strategies

Prearrest (Primary Prevention)	Arrest (Arrest Referral, Intake/Detention)	Adjudication — Case Filing, Pretrial Release/Detention	Adjudication — Trial/Adjudication, Sentencing/Disposition	Disposition (Sanction, Sentence Modification)	Postdisposition (Aftercare)
Intervention options/strategies • Early interventions by child care professionals (health care, education, social services) based on risk factors for delinquency • Social services agency interventions to address problematic child-rearing practices in community/home • Interventions to change community norms about violence (public information campaigns)	*Intervention options/strategies* • Emergency mental health/detox services • Crisis intervention services • Law enforcement diversion programs • Intake and assessment services	*Intervention options/strategies:* • Intake release screening • Community supervision • Electronic monitoring • Day reporting • Home detention • Attendant care • Pretrial residential programs (emergency foster or shelter care, staff secure detention, secure detention) • Mental health and substance abuse services	*Intervention options/strategies:* • Youth and family evaluation services • Diversion programs • Dispute resolution/mediation programs • Continued out-of-home care during adjudication (emergency foster or shelter care, staff secure detention, secure detention) • Continued access to mental health and substance abuse services during adjudication	*Intervention options/strategies:* • Restitution/community service • Community supervision/case management • Intensive community supervision • Electronic monitoring • Day reporting • Alternative education programs • Job training/placement services • Mediation/victim reconciliation • Counseling • Mentoring • Substance abuse treatment • Family support services • Work programs • Residential program as a dispositional placement (halfway houses, foster and group homes, residential treatment) • Independent living services	*Intervention options/strategies:* • Reentry services and programs (disposition options/strategies configured for successful reentry on release from secure facility)

Aftercare Programs

Small Community-Based Secure Facility

Use of intervention options and strategies can reduce reliance on secure confinement. This model reserves secure placement for the small number of offenders who pose a threat to public safety or who are unsuitable for alternative settings or programs.

All youth coming in contact with the juvenile justice system

Source: S. Zavlek, JPFYouth

Steps in the Juvenile Justice System Assessment Process

1. Develop a community profile. Describe the following characteristics of the community:

- Geographic area: location, size, climate, land use, etc.

- Resident population: demographic breakdowns (age, gender, income, marital status, educational attainment, etc.); population projections.

- Economy: major industry, economic trends, unemployment levels, poverty levels, etc.

- Assets and infrastructure: recreational facilities, libraries, shopping, transportation systems, health care, etc.

Such a profile yields information about issues and trends in the community that may affect use of juvenile detention or correctional facilities.

2. Develop a profile of the existing juvenile justice system. Describe the juvenile justice resources currently available in the jurisdiction, including the following:

- Police department.

- Court services, including probation and any alternative dispute resolution approaches.

- Prosecution and defense bar.

- Juvenile detention and placement facilities and operations.

- Community programs for juvenile offenders (day reporting, electronic monitoring, community service, mediation, etc.).

These descriptions should include information about each entity's functions, staffing, funding levels and sources, workload, etc. They should also highlight any major deficiencies or concerns with regard to facilities and operations.

3. Assess other community resources. Describe all other community resources that may work cooperatively with the justice system, including the following:

- Emergency services: fire, EMS, etc.

- Healthcare services: including services provided to juvenile offenders in the community and in custody.

- Mental health and substance abuse services: including services provided to juvenile offenders in the community and in custody (both residential and nonresidential).

- Juvenile services: residential and nonresidential.

- Social services.

- Schools and other providers of educational services.

These descriptions should include information about the extent to which each entity serves the juvenile offender population or otherwise addresses justice system needs. They should highlight barriers or problems encountered in providing services to this population.

Continued on page 14

Continued from page 13

4. Develop baseline information about how the sanctioning system currently operates. Address the following questions:

- What is happening in various sanctioning components for preadjudicated and adjudicated youth: detention, placement, intermediate sanctions, preadjudication services, diversion programs, probation and parole?

- How are cases being processed through the juvenile justice system, and what is the level and nature of coordination among justice system agencies?

- What is the system's current capacity for collecting and compiling information to support policy development efforts?

- Will the political climate support or impede change?

This information should help planners create or refine written policies regarding desired outcomes, target offender populations, screening procedures, intervention approaches, and capacity and costs of individual sanctions within the existing continuum of services.

5. Research historical justice system trends and analyze data. Collect and analyze the following types of data:

- Law enforcement data: arrests, rearrests, offense types, use of citations and warrants, etc.

- Court data: case filings, types of charges, dispositions, failure to appear rates, bonding practices, etc.

- Detention data: admissions and releases, average daily population, average length of stay, offender profile (age, gender, education, employment, special needs, charges, charge status, charge type, etc), recidivism, etc.

- Probation data: commitments and discharges, revocation data, caseloads, etc.

- Use of alternatives to incarceration: number and types of alternatives, number of juvenile offenders served, program completion/failure rates, etc.

Planners should also gather information from justice system officials regarding their policies and practices that affect use of detention. It can be helpful to construct a caseflow diagram as part of this process to understand how juveniles move through the system. The diagram provides a framework for linking together data from the various components of the system. As these data are collected and analyzed, a better understanding of the capabilities, deficiencies, and needs of the current system begins to emerge (Burke, Cushman, and Ney, 1996).

System Master Plan

The information compiled and analyzed in the assessment should be developed into a master plan that encompasses the design, use, capacity, and cost of a coordinated system of juvenile justice sanctions and services. A primary goal of this strategic plan is to identify opportunities for addressing inefficiencies and needs so that the system will function better and management of services and bedspace utilization can improve.

Through this process, states and local jurisdictions can evaluate whether juvenile correctional beds are being used appropriately and whether more effective use of alternatives might have an impact on the number or type of beds required. Jurisdictions can also determine the need for bedspace in smaller, specialized facilities that can be responsive to management needs of special populations such as sex offenders, female offenders, and youth with mental health, substance abuse, and/or behavior disorders.

The Facility Development Process

The process of developing a new secure facility for juvenile offenders (figure 3) is fundamentally similar to the process of creating a master plan for the overall juvenile justice system. Both activities rely on a systematic, participatory approach.

Just as a system master plan defines system needs and opportunities for the future, a facility master plan defines the functional and space needs of a new facility. To lay a solid foundation for the facility master planning process, stakeholders should achieve a consensus on the shared values, vision, mission, goals, and objectives for the new facility. Ideally, this process will be informed by comprehensive data on the justice system and the juvenile population to be served, developed through the assessment of the overall system.

Building a Foundation for Planning a Facility

The first step in the facility planning process is building a foundation for planning. In taking this first step, it is helpful to keep in mind that the best way to ensure the success of a project is to take control of it from start to finish. This requires understanding the decisionmaking processes that will be used and identifying and empowering the right participants so they can make sound and timely decisions. It also requires understanding facility planning, design, and construction processes; knowing how to create budgets and how to meet goals within limited budgets; and understanding the roles and responsibilities of all parties, including the owner.[9]

Develop the Project Approach and Participatory Process

The key to building and operating a successful small, community-based facility (or network of facilities) is a concerned, informed, and engaged owner and community. The facility planning process should be active and participatory. This approach creates a sense of shared ownership by all participants in the process, promotes an informed consensus, and helps to ensure that the needs of all interested parties and their departments and units are addressed.

A planning team is established to carry out the day-to-day work of developing a master plan for the proposed facility. The composition of this team depends on the jurisdiction and the facility, but, typically, the team includes key facility staff (e.g., administrators and managers), technical members (e.g., an architect and a professional planner), and security and law enforcement representatives. For a community-based center, the planning team should also include court administrators, teachers, health professionals, and other applicable specialists. The planning committee is extremely "hands-on" and active throughout the facility development process.

Analyze the Population Served

Jurisdictions planning to build new secure juvenile facilities should first carefully examine their juvenile offender populations and the classification systems being used to determine secure bedspace needs. This analysis (which may have been substantially completed as part of the system assessment) should identify any existing alternatives to secure detention and placement and determine whether these alternatives are being used effectively. New space should be built only for youth who cannot function safely and effectively in less restrictive alternative programs.

---

[9] The term "owner" refers to the organization or system that has primary responsibility for operating and paying for the facility. Depending on the jurisdiction, this could be a state, a county, an American Indian tribe, the juvenile court, or the probation department. The owner is also the entity that will occupy and operate the new facility when it is complete.

Figure 3. Facility Development

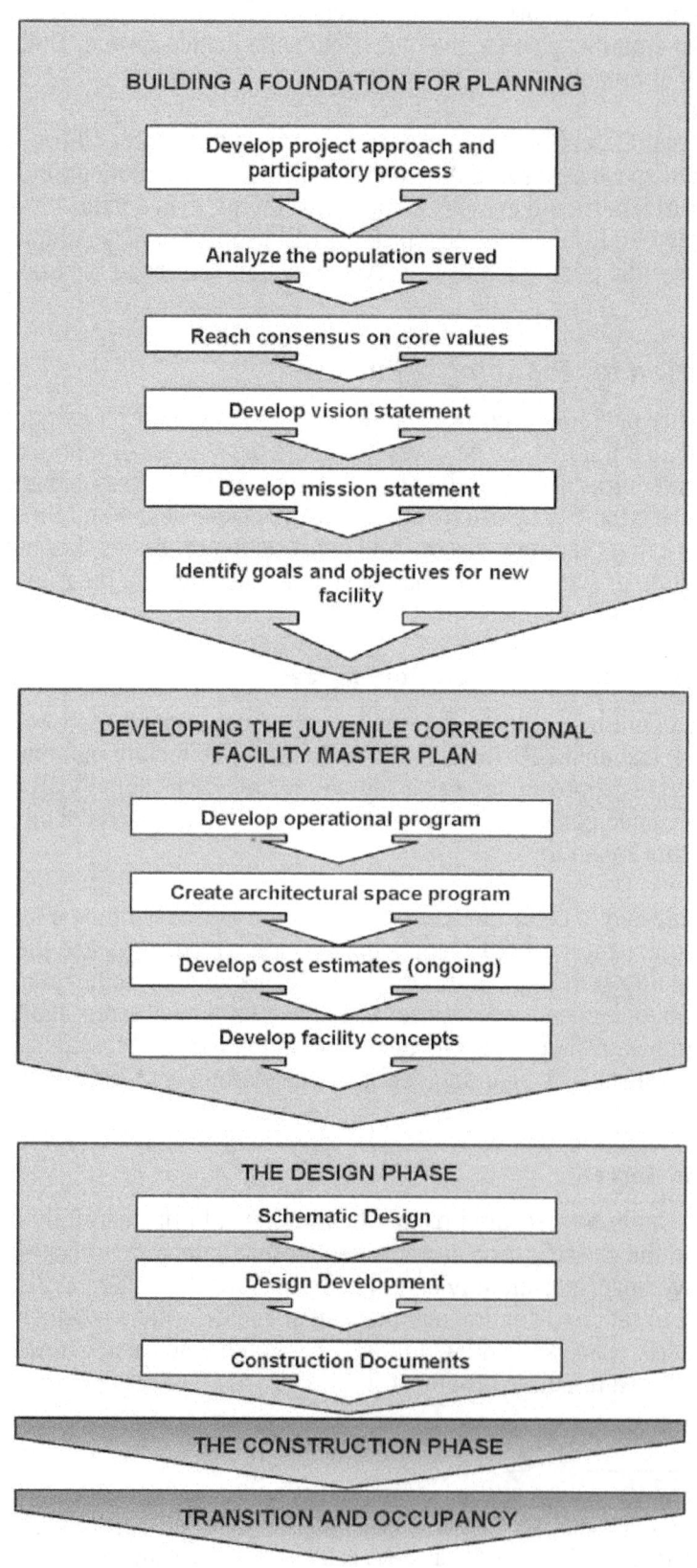

Source: S. Zavlek, IPFYouth

Population Profile

The first step in this analysis is to profile the current population of youth in the juvenile justice system and existing facilities. This involves gathering and analyzing data on age, gender, offense, legal status, offense history, substance abuse history, behavior, academic level, family, living arrangement at time of arrest, gang affiliation, and special management needs. Profiles should be based on the most comprehensive and recent local data available. Random samples may be used in populous jurisdictions, but larger samples and analyses of all data are warranted in jurisdictions with smaller populations of juvenile offenders.

The profile information is combined with population projections to determine: (1) appropriate custodial and noncustodial programs/alternatives for all youth, and approximate numbers of youth in each; (2) the types of custodial and noncustodial facilities that are needed and appropriate for youth and programs; (3) classification of youth in existing correctional facilities; and (4) design features of all spaces, from classrooms to living units, that best support youth and programs.

The profiling process can help jurisdictions determine both the need to build new facilities and the types of new facilities to build. For example, the data may indicate that a jurisdiction needs a 40-bed secure facility[10] for boys, a 24-bed secure facility for girls, a 32-bed staff-secure facility[11] for boys, and 4 multiservice community centers (without beds) to provide substance abuse treatment, academic tutoring, anger management, family counseling, and prevocational training for 400 youth. A facility that targets the most serious and chronic juvenile offenders should be considered only after a jurisdiction verifies that the number of juveniles projected to fall within the physically secure facility category justifies construction of a new facility.

System Factors

In analyzing bedspace needs, planners should consider recent or pending juvenile justice system developments—legislative changes, policy shifts, crime trends, and other factors—at the local, state, and (to a lesser extent) national levels. One example is legislation that allows (or requires) juveniles older than a certain age who commit certain offenses to be charged as adults. Such a policy may reduce the number of local juvenile commitment beds needed but, because trials in the adult system often take longer than juvenile court proceedings, may increase the number of detention beds needed for youth with cases pending adjudication. Another example of legislation that affected bed needs is the federal Juvenile Justice and Delinquency Prevention Act of 1974, which required the deinstitutionalization of status offenders. Fewer low-security beds were needed, but this reduction was more than offset by the increase in demand during the 1980s and early 1990s for more secure bedspace to accommodate accused and adjudicated juveniles (e.g., youth adjudicated under legislation instituting harsher sentencing requirements and more severe treatment of serious juvenile offenders).

Although awareness of such developments is important, the continuum of available services and sanctions available for young offenders has an even greater impact on bedspace needs. Before a jurisdiction decides on the number and types of beds to be built, it should thoroughly study the population profile and projections together with existing and possible noncustodial alternatives. Without this key step, the jurisdiction is likely to overbuild, and the result will be dramatically higher construction, operating, and life-cycle costs than are necessary.

---

[10] Secure facility in this context refers to a physically restricting environment that has hard construction, locked doors, and a secure perimeter.

[11] "Staff-secure" refers to an environment that is restricted by intensive staff supervision rather than by physical restrictions.

Facility Bedspace Capacity

Once a jurisdiction justifies the need to build a new facility, the next step is to calculate the bedspace capacity required for the target population. Because bedspace capacity has a direct impact on facility size, staffing, and operating and construction costs, establishing the number of beds required initially and over the next 10 to 20 years is a critical part of the planning process. Planners should be careful to document the rationale for all bedspace decisions.

Bed needs are determined by multiplying offender population projections by a factor that accounts for peaking and classification. Accounting for peaking is necessary because facilities must be able to handle fluctuations in offender populations. Classification must be considered to provide enough beds for different population categories and to ensure appropriate housing unit characteristics, which may vary widely depending on offender age, gender, offense, and behaviors. For example, if a violent, out-of-control youth enters a facility that has only general-population beds, serious problems may result. Although such youth usually comprise a very small percentage of the overall juvenile offender population, their impact on facility operations can be dramatic unless the facility design anticipates and accommodates their requirements.

Reach Consensus on Core Values

One of the most critical steps in building a foundation for facility planning is the articulation of core principles or values for the new facility. The core values, which reflect the shared beliefs of all stakeholders in the facility development process, will guide all decisions and activities related to planning, designing, and, ultimately, operating the new facility. These values help the owner define boundaries for decisions and activities and provide a gauge for keeping the planning and design processes on track.

Core values help the jurisdiction define a vision for the facility and a mission that will move the jurisdiction toward that vision. The mission and all related actions should fall within the boundaries defined by the core values. For example, if a core value is "promoting partnerships with family," then the facility's policies and design should be consistent with that value. It would allow frequent enough visits to accommodate families' varying personal demands and work schedules. Visiting rules and procedures would be clearly stated. The facility would be designed to welcome family and guests by making access easy and providing comfortable and appropriate visiting spaces.

Develop the Vision Statement

The vision statement for a new facility will guide the planning process and provide the foundation for the facility's operational and space requirements. The statement should be far reaching, portraying a future state

---

Sample Statements of Core Values

Promoting public safety. We promote public safety by being part of a continuum of services for youth that begins with prevention and ends with successful reintegration into the community.

Providing a purposeful program for youth. We provide a comprehensive, structured, purposeful, and gender-specific program that develops assets in youth and promotes their successful reintegration into the community.

Promoting partnerships with family. We encourage collaborations with family to best meet the needs of youth in our care and their families/support networks and to facilitate their successful transition back into the community.

Promoting partnerships with businesses, government, and community-based organizations. We encourage strong links and collaborations with business leaders, government, and the community to best meet the needs of youth in our care.

Promoting staff professionalism. We believe that staff are a valuable resource entitled to a supportive work environment that equitably enhances professional development and recognizes excellence.

Sample Vision Statement

All youth in the care of the Juvenile Justice Center will reach their fullest potential in a safe and nurturing environment and will become capable, productive, and law-abiding citizens.

that is better in some significant way than the current state. It should envision the new facility as part of a paradigm for juvenile crime control and treatment that taps into the community's strengths to address recidivism and reduce crime. Developing the vision statement requires a high level of participatory planning among key stakeholders. Ideally, before stakeholders begin this task, a system assessment team, legislative body, or umbrella agency will have created a broader vision for the juvenile justice system as a whole that provides a context for the facility's vision.

Develop the Mission Statement

The mission statement defines the "vehicle" that will transport the jurisdiction from its present state to its vision. It usually answers three questions:

♦ What is the purpose of the facility?

♦ What clients does the facility serve?

♦ What activities, services, or resources does the facility provide?

The mission statement should reflect the facility's core values, local risk factors for delinquency and youth crime, and community strengths and resources. It should be based on a consensus of all stakeholders.

Together, the statements of the facility's core values, vision, and mission provide a roadmap for key decisions during the planning process—including the definition of goals and objectives. In the longer term, these three fundamental statements will influence the nature and scope of juvenile offender custody, care, and treatment.

> **Sample Mission Statement**
>
> The mission of the Juvenile Justice Center is to promote public safety, reduce recidivism, and rehabilitate youth in our care through a continuum of services that are provided in safe and nurturing environments. To achieve this mission, the Juvenile Justice Center will focus on providing:
>
> - Purposeful programming that includes prevention, diversion, supervision, education, behavioral management, therapy, youth accountability, and transitional services.
>
> - Partnerships with families, the community, business leaders, and government.
>
> - A diverse, well-trained, professional staff.

Identify Goals and Objectives

The goals and objectives of a facility shape its specific programmatic and design elements. Goals should support or build on the community's strengths and address local risk factors for delinquency and youth crime.[12] Therefore, the process of defining the facility's goals and objectives begins with a review of these strengths and risk factors. The available continuum of services and sanctions identified during the system assessment is a critical part of the protective factors or strengths from which the jurisdiction can draw. A new facility should be designed to build on the jurisdiction's strengths or protective factors (e.g., by providing safe and accessible workspaces for probation officers, lawyers, community-based service providers, and aftercare program staff operating in the facility) and to address its most prevalent risk factors (e.g., by providing comprehensive programming and well-planned spaces to support academic and counseling programs).

Goals often are expressed as the reduction of juvenile problem behaviors (e.g., recidivism, drug and alcohol abuse), reduction of risk factors (e.g., family conflict, availability of alcohol and drugs), or

---

[12] Research indicates that exposure to certain "risk factors" at the community, peer group, individual, family, or school level results in a significantly higher likelihood that a youth will become involved in delinquency, illegal drug use, or crime. The same research has identified "protective factors" or "assets" that appear to buffer youth against the effects of exposure to multiple risk factors. This research finds that strategies to decrease risk factors and enhance protective factors are important elements of an overall strategy for delinquency prevention and intervention (Hawkins et al, 2000; Loeber and Farrington, 1998; Farrington, 1996; Howell, 1995).

enhancement of protective factors (e.g., strong bonds between children and prosocial members of the community). Goals represent the desired end, not the means to the end. For example, if "lack of skills for employment" is identified as a risk factor for delinquency, the corresponding goal could be "helping youth in the facility gain skills that would increase their employability."

Each goal should have a number of specific operational or programmatic objectives associated with it. Objectives are stated in concrete terms. Generally they specify who or what will change, by how much, and over what period of time. The more specific the objectives, the easier it is to determine if and when they have been achieved. For example, if a goal is "reducing family conflict," an associated objective might be "Within 6 months after the facility begins operations, 85 percent of youth in its care for more than 10 days will be engaged in a family counseling program."

As noted, each goal and objective has programmatic and design implications. During the facility master planning process (discussed further below), planners should conduct workshops with relevant staff and administrators to program each area of the facility, to ensure that the design will help staff achieve their identified goals and objectives. For example, to reach the goal of an enhanced family counseling program, the facility owner may choose to hire additional social workers or retain an independent contractor to set up an intensive family counseling program. The facility design would need to include spaces to accommodate the program. Such spaces might include a number of small conference rooms that are easily accessible to families, counselors, and residents and "family-friendly" visiting areas. Creating family-friendly visiting areas might have implications for where the areas are located (indoors or outdoors, accessible to visitors' entrance); how they are designed (features to provide privacy, comfort, safety); and their functional and visual qualities (light, colors, visibility).

By carefully defining goals and objectives that are consistent with the facility's core values, vision, and mission, planners can ensure that the core values are expressed in specific design features (figure 4).

Developing the Facility Master Plan

Once the system assessment is complete and the foundation for facility planning is in place—the core values, vision, mission, goals, and objectives—the next step is to develop the facility master plan. The master plan is not an isolated document. It should be viewed within the context of the overall plan for juvenile justice system sanctions and services.

As with overall system planning, the process of developing a master plan for a juvenile correctional facility is a participatory one. In addition to the interested stakeholders and the owner's steering committee and planning team, the process involves consultants, architects, engineers, builders, and the public. In developing the facility master plan, participants will rely on the values, vision, mission, goals, and objectives already identified for the new facility and will explore operational and spatial alternatives to ensure the best possible configuration to achieve the mission and goals and realize the vision for the facility. The following sections provide a step-by-step overview of the facility master planning process, together with practical tips for implementing the process.

Develop the Operational Program

The operational program is a detailed narrative description of the specific program and service requirements, operational procedures, and management practices for each functional area of the facility. New facilities offer jurisdictions an opportunity to improve operations and services as defined during the system assessment process. Jurisdictions can explore state-of-the-art and emerging treatment and management methods that are responsive to the diverse needs of today's youth-serving agencies.

Figure 4. Translating Core Values, Goals, and Objectives Into Design Features: Illustrations From a Facility Planning Project

Sample Core Values	Related Goal	Objective	Selected Implications for Facility Design
Promoting public safety	Develop a facility design that protects the public by preventing security breaches from within while permitting safe, secure, broad access for visitors.	In the first year of operation, the facility will have no escapes and will reduce reported incidents in visiting areas by 80%.	Maximum-secure facility perimeter with graduated levels of secure circulation within the facility to optimize safe and secure access by visitors. Strategically placed cameras at points of ingress and egress, good visual access to circulation corridors and visiting areas.
Providing a purposeful program for youth	Assist youth in developing a more positive self-image.	Within 10 days of admission, all youth will be engaged in a behavior management system that creates opportunities for success by permitting youth to achieve increasing levels of responsibility and privilege.	Availability of housing units ranging from maximum secure to transitional, elite lounges, isolation rooms, yards and courtyards, and diverse program spaces; design features such as desks and manual light switches (with overrides) in bedrooms; excellent site lines to allow movement to program spaces with visual observation.
Promoting partnerships with family	Encourage more and healthier family involvement with resident youth.	Upon activation, visiting hours will be increased 50%, with a commensurate increase in family visits; by the end of the first year of operation, 50% of eligible families will be enrolled in family counseling programs with residents in the facility.	Extensive, diverse, safe visiting spaces; conference and meeting rooms located conveniently for regularly scheduled family counseling sessions that include youth, social workers, and family members; large and small group visitation rooms; soft colors; privacy; child-friendly spaces in visiting area.
Promoting partnerships with local businesses, government, and community-based organizations	Increase residents' marketable skills.	All eligible youth in the school program will have access to vocational programs designed to teach marketable skills linked to the local economy.	Spaces designed for vocational programs tied to certifications in trades that are supported by the local economy or specific industries or businesses within the region. Participation of staff of related industries or businesses in facility planning and design process. Safe and easy access to vocational education and other education spaces for visiting instructors.

Source: S. Zavlek, IPFYouth

Jurisdictions can also investigate various classification systems, security levels, and daily program alternatives. In addition to accommodating traditional elements such as housing, dining, education, and recreation areas, a newly designed physical setting can incorporate new types of programs appropriate for special populations, units with smaller bed capacities, youth transitioning to the community, and even nonresident youth and their families (e.g., outpatient services, walk-in counseling, community supervision and training, conflict resolution, skills development, ombudsman services). A small, regional or community-based facility designed along these lines can provide support services to youth after their release from the facility, to youth who have been in custody in out-of-state programs, or to siblings of youth in custody who may be at high risk of becoming involved in the juvenile justice system.

The process of defining functional requirements for the operational program should be guided by the concepts and goals established during system assessment and planning and by the core values, vision, mission, goals, and objectives that constitute the foundation for facility planning. The best facilities are developed in response to a clear vision defined long before physical design efforts begin. The values that underlie that vision, established early on, serve as the benchmark for evaluating all aspects of the physical design process.

Before physical design efforts get underway, operational programming defines the kinds of spaces and the amount of space that will best serve the functions envisioned for the facility. This process involves rigorous examination of all potential activities (housing, education, vocational training, visiting, dining, recreation, medical services, administration, admissions, and support services); exploration of alternative approaches; and detailed description of the approaches determined to be most responsive to operational priorities.

Tips: Functional Requirements

Input from appropriate officials and staff is necessary in identifying the functional requirements of a new facility. Consultants can help to gather this input via questionnaires, interviews, and workshops.

Planners should work with interested stakeholders to define each functional area (e.g., intake, food service, recreation) in terms of the following:

- Mission, objectives, and policy issues defining the purpose of the area.

- General uses, including anticipated activities and functions.

- Frequent users (staff, students, community groups, neighborhood residents).

- Access (private, secure, and public movement) and adjacencies (which areas should be located adjacent or close to the functional area).

- Security level, including use of security hardware and cameras; sightlines, building materials (e.g., hollow metal doors versus solid wood doors, porcelain versus stainless steel bathroom fixtures, cement block versus dry wall); and furniture and finishes (e.g., fixed versus loose furniture, bright versus soft colors, carpet versus tile).

- Group size and supervision methods (e.g., housing unit capacity, direct or indirect supervision, spaces to support activities, and, if applicable, behavior management programs).

- Behavioral considerations, including users' perceptions, emotions, or circumstances (e.g., youth's high stress level and potential volatility in the intake area).

- Staffing requirements (direct care and other staff needed in the space, by shift and day of week).

- Hours of operation (including days of the week that the area will be in use and peak usage hours).

- Design directives (design features of each area, discrete spaces for users, special equipment, and furnishings).

- Applicable codes and standards.

Create the Architectural Space Program

Once operational needs are known, space planning begins. The architectural space program translates the functional requirements developed in the operational program into space, or square footage, requirements for each functional area of the facility and for the building as a whole. It defines with specificity the type and number of spaces required to support each function. The amount of square footage required for individual areas depends on a number of factors, including the kind of activity involved, the number and characteristics of juveniles who may use the space, staffing requirements, good operating practices,

---

Tips: Square Footage Estimates

The architectural space program should include a program summary that provides a tally of the net square footage (NSF) and gross square footage (GSF) totals for each functional area (e.g., housing, intake, food service, etc.) of the facility. The NSF represents assignable or usable floor space and excludes corridors, stairs, elevators, mechanical spaces, walls, and the building structure itself. The GSF equals the NSF multiplied by efficiency factors that represent the ratio of net usable space to gross unassignable space. Each functional area has its own efficiency factor. For example, in a recreation area comprising a large gymnasium, a storage room, and an office, the percentage of usable space would be high and therefore the efficiency factor would be low. The opposite would be true of a high-security, single-occupancy housing unit, which has a large quantity of walls (bedroom, bathroom, storage, etc.), plumbing chases, and secure construction.

In estimating total building GSF, some architects and planners add up all the GSF amounts for the various functional areas; others multiply the GSF sum by a building efficiency factor, which accounts for circulation among functional areas and mechanical and electrical areas that serve the entire building. In the latter case, lower multipliers are usually used for each functional area of the facility. As a result, the estimated total GSF for the building would be similar using either approach.

---

required furniture and equipment, and relevant state and national standards. Evaluation of these factors generates net area, or square footage, requirements for the usable areas of each anticipated facility function. Net area requirements are then combined with space requirements for general circulation and resident and staff movement through the facility, mechanical rooms, electrical closets, and other structural elements such as wall thickness. This calculation generates the gross square footage (GSF) or total building area of the facility.

The space requirements in the architectural program and all of the factors examined to derive them are the basis for space organization activities, specifically the development of adjacency diagrams that illustrate the desired connections and relationships between individual spaces (e.g., bedrooms, bathrooms, and living areas in housing units) and between groups of spaces (e.g., housing and education areas). The adjacency diagrams indicate general access and circulation patterns, resident movement, control points, and security features. Because the relationship and proximity of the various areas can be critical to the effective functioning of the facility, the design should clearly reflect the desired connections indicated in the adjacency diagrams.

Tips: Adjacency Information

One way to convey adjacency information is to create a matrix that lists all functional spaces in the facility along both the top and the left side. Each box in the matrix represents two corresponding spaces. In each box, a number represents the ideal relationship between the two spaces (one number might represent "must be immediately adjacent," another "visibility from one space to the other, but no physical connection"). Alternatively, "bubble" diagrams can illustrate relationships between functional spaces and activity areas (both indoor and outdoor) and the necessary or desirable features of each activity area.

Develop Cost Estimates

The area narratives, building gross square footage, and general spatial relationships described in the previous sections are used to project initial construction costs and total project development costs. The construction cost usually represents about 75 percent of the total cost of a project, with the remaining 25 percent covering items such as architectural and engineering fees, furnishings, site work, and contingencies. Thus, a building that costs $10 million will usually entail a total project development cost of $13.5 million.

Tips: Accuracy in Estimating Construction Costs

To calculate construction costs for the entire building, the cost estimator may simply use an average cost per square foot for all components combined, or the estimator may assign each component a different cost per square foot that reflects various factors. (For example, the cost per square foot for a high-security unit will always be relatively high, whereas that for nonsecure classrooms and administrative space will always be relatively low.) This second approach usually results in more accurate cost estimates.

If initial projections surpass anticipated or mandated funding levels (see section on funding considerations, below), further space programming is necessary to explore alternatives. Because it is difficult and expensive to make changes once the architect has begun to develop building plans, these cost considerations should be resolved as early in the process as is practical.

Tips: Ongoing Budget Review

As the planning and design process continues, the cost estimator has more and more information about the new building. Hence, each subsequent cost estimate should be more accurate than the preceding one. Each time a cost estimate is developed, decisionmakers should check that the project is still within budget. If an estimate exceeds the budget, planners should find ways to lower costs before entering the next phase of the process.

Ideally, project funding will be established at the completion of the programming process so that the size and anticipated cost of the facility have been thoroughly analyzed before the facility design process begins. Establishing the budget before programming takes place may make it necessary to eliminate required areas or reduce capacity if projected costs exceed the budget.

Tips: Staffing Costs

In addition to design and construction costs, planners must consider the cost of operating the facility. Staffing costs constitute the lion's share of a facility's annual operating costs and life-cycle costs (about 70 percent of life-cycle costs over 30 years). Thus, controlling staffing costs is a major consideration in facility planning. To estimate these costs, jurisdictions should develop a generic staffing plan based on a general assumption about the number of housing units and the number and type of posts, programs, and services projected for the facility. It is critical to consider how services will be provided (e.g., centralized versus decentralized, contracted or owner-operated). Developing a realistic staffing plan driven by actual programming and operational needs requires input not only from the facility operator and consultants but also from managers and staff of each functional area of the facility.

Develop Facility Concepts

The architect develops facility concepts (or conceptual diagrams) primarily to help the owner choose the design option that is most consistent with the jurisdiction's values, site, needs, and budget. These diagrams provide a visual representation of various configurations that may meet functional and space requirements. They illustrate key elements such as the facility "footprint" and the configuration of housing units and other functional areas. The diagrams should reflect issues pertaining to housing unit size, centralized versus decentralized services, classification divisions, access and circulation, and security.

In this phase, the architect and planner determine how many stories the facility will have and which functions work on which stories (blocking and stacking). They may also do studies that use three-dimensional forms to examine the relation of the building to its surrounding context and with its subparts (massing), to reach decisions about the building's external architectural form. By exploring conceptual alternatives in this way, the architect and planner can find an overall best solution.

Developing several facility concepts serves a number of purposes. In addition to depicting the various design options in a way that is meaningful for justice system professionals and other participants in the planning process, the concepts are useful in site planning, cost estimating (see previous section), and staffing.

Tips: Facility Concepts and Site Planning

If the jurisdiction has already selected a site (or has narrowed its selection to a few sites), the facility concepts should be applied to the site or sites. In addition to the building itself, the site concepts should show the following:

- Access points for general vehicular and pedestrian traffic, law enforcement (including secure ingress and egress), correctional agency vehicles, delivery vehicles (including loading docks), and trash vehicles.

- Outdoor recreational areas.

- Areas for the building to expand (e.g., added housing and classrooms).

- Areas for functions that may be added to the facility in the future (e.g., juvenile or family courts, day treatment centers, alternative schools, clubs).

After studying the concepts, the owner probably will prefer one option but will want to see some modifications. The architect refines the preferred concept based on owner input, and the process continues until the owner approves the design. A more detailed cost estimate should then be developed for the selected design concept.

Design

The building design process takes place following completion of the facility master plan. During building design, the owner works closely with the architect to ensure that the proposed design reflects the values, principles, and facility features identified during the planning process.

The design phase proceeds in three stages: schematic design, design development, and production of the construction documents.

Schematic Design

The schematic design builds on the selected facility concepts and continues to rely on the architectural space program and adjacency requirements. In schematic drawings, the owner can see the relative shapes and sizes of all the spaces in the facility. The main circulation patterns and the general character of the building begin to emerge in the schematic design phase.

The end products of the schematic design phase include floor plans, site plans, a security zone plan, a site circulation plan, building sections, and elevations. The architect and engineer also outline the basic structural, electrical, and mechanical building systems and basic interior and exterior finishes and colors (usually referred to as "outline specifications").

Approval of the schematic drawings is a major step for the owner, who should insist that the architect circulate the schematic drawings widely and discuss them before panels that include all levels of facility staff and other stakeholders and interested parties. The architect should be willing to make several presentations at this stage to explain the basic concepts and ideas behind the design. Once the schematic design phase is complete, a more detailed and accurate cost estimate can be generated.

Design Development

During design development, detailed drawings and specifications are produced. These include finalized floor plans, elevations, and sections. The architects also develop drawings that show details such as staircases, windows, and doors. All design development drawings are drawn to scale.

Design development is the first phase in which the full spectrum of engineers—mechanical, electrical, electronics/security, plumbing, structural—are heavily involved. They produce drawings that show structure, lighting, electrical outlets, electronics, plumbing, heating/ventilation/air conditioning (HVAC) systems, and construction materials. Specifications for all building systems, materials, and finishes outlined during the schematic design phase are detailed during this phase.

Tips: Critical Tasks for Owners During Design Development

- **Provide input on hardware, materials, and equipment.** This information is then indicated on the drawings and specifications. The owner should help to ensure that these items are consistent with the facility's mission and day-to-day operations and with the profile of the youth who will use the facility. In providing this input, the owner should keep in mind that different areas (even different housing units) probably will require different types of doors, windows, flooring materials, plumbing fixtures, finishes, etc. Owners should solicit input from facility managers and staff, architects, engineers, and maintenance administrators.

- **Discuss safety and security implications with the project's security consultant.**

- **Ensure that the project is within budget and on track.** If the project is not within budget, "value engineering" may be necessary. At this point in the process, it is easier to change materials, finishes, plumbing fixtures, hardware, etc., than to change or delete spaces. One exception: Some areas may be designed with the option of including them if the budget permits or adding them later if necessary (e.g., if a facility is designed with six housing units, perhaps one or two could be added in the future).

Construction Documents

Once design development is complete, the architect and engineers produce the detailed working documents that will be used for obtaining competitive construction bids and for construction. Their final submission includes working drawings for architecture and all engineering disciplines, a full set of specifications, and a construction schedule. At the end of this phase, they also submit a final revised cost estimate for construction.

Construction

Once the construction drawings are ready, the project is offered for bidding. Contractors submit bids in sealed envelopes, the bids are opened and compared, and, if the bids are consistent with the project framework, the jurisdiction begins negotiations, usually starting with the lowest responsive bidder. Some bidders may be eliminated based on criteria established by the owner and design team (e.g., recent experience building correctional facilities, or sufficient bonding/insurance). Once the negotiations are complete, the jurisdiction signs a detailed contract with the successful bidder.

Tips: The Design/Build Option

The design/build approach is an alternative to the traditional construction bidding process. In design/build, which is a form of project delivery that aims to simplify and speed up construction, owners contract with a single entity—the design-builder—to provide both design and construction services. The design-build entity may be a single firm, a group of experts, or a joint venture. Typically, the team includes an architect and a contractor, who may be partners in the undertaking or one a subcontractor to the other. Principal advantages of a design/build contract are the single point of responsibility and the potential to combine otherwise independent phases and thereby save time and money. A downside may be a reduction in the owner's responsibility and involvement after a certain point. To minimize loss of decisionmaking and control in such an arrangement, owners sometimes have one design team carry a project through schematic design or even partially into design development and then offer the project to design/builders for bids, specifying that the design cannot be changed and the outline specifications must be followed.

Once the contract is signed, construction begins. Timely, high-quality construction requires a good construction manager and effective supervision by the architect/designer (e.g., through approval of shop drawings, reports from observation of construction, interpretation of contract documents, and punch lists). However, the jurisdiction should continue to have its own project manager—ideally someone with a background in construction or architecture—during this phase.

Transition

While design and construction are moving forward, the owner carefully prepares for transition to and operation of the new facility. A well-thought-out transition and activation plan can help to ensure that staff and residents make a smooth transition and that the new facility operates as effectively and efficiently as possible.

The transition process, which requires attention to many details ranging from ensuring safety and security to supplying an adequate number of wastebaskets, is complex, time consuming, and demanding on staff. The process should begin 18 to 24 months before the projected completion date for construction.

The first step in the transition process is to establish an organizational structure. This includes appointing a transition coordinator and team, identifying major transition tasks and goals, and establishing task forces. The transition team should include representatives of all key facility functions (e.g., administration, training, programs, plant management, education). The steering committee formed earlier in the facility planning process will also continue to play a role. This initial step also involves defining a hierarchy of authority for decisionmaking and a process for identifying issues and getting them addressed.

Tips: Transition Task Forces

Task forces for carrying out the transition to a new facility typically include the following:

- Construction monitoring.
- Furniture, fixtures, and equipment.
- Interagency coordination.
- Programming.
- Scenarios, staffing, and facility schedule.
- Policies, procedures, and post orders.
- Security.
- Computerization and communications.

- Move management.
- Transportation.
- Public affairs and community relations.
- Recruitment, selection, and training of new and existing staff.
- Transition and operating budget.
- Resident and staff orientation.

The transition coordinator should establish a master timeline for the overall transition process. Each task force should have a detailed action plan and a timeline. The action plans (which are fluid) should clearly identify all tasks to be completed, due dates, and people responsible for each task.

Toward the end of construction and after the facility is officially transferred from the general contractor to the owner, the owner increasingly controls the project and must complete some essential tasks. An owner's "punchlist" should identify items overlooked by the contractor (e.g., missing locks, unpainted corners, building materials left behind) and address items that may create safety or security breaches (e.g., blind spots, fixtures that create suicide risks). A detailed logistical plan for the move should be developed, tested, and scheduled. Facility systems should be tested, and staff should receive training from manufacturers or staff trainers on how to operate these systems. Owner-purchased furniture, equipment, and supplies should be received and installed, and outfitting of the facility should be completed.

While attending to the many details involved in making the transition to the new facility, jurisdictions should keep the "big picture" in mind. A new physical environment offers a unique opportunity to implement major improvements in operations. Jurisdictions should, where possible, dedicate the time, effort, and resources necessary to take full advantage of that opportunity.

Tips: Smooth Transition to a Smaller Facility

Making the transition from large congregate care facilities to smaller facilities will inevitably present both challenges and advantages. The result can be disappointing if effective plans for operating the new facility are not in place. The following considerations are essential to a smooth transition:

- **Identify and resolve old problems.** Planners should provide well-thought-out programming, support facility staff through good training programs, and remember the adage that "buildings don't solve problems, people do."

- **Staff buy-in.** All levels of staff should be involved in developing operational plans. Staff committees can look at specific areas—security, education, food services, visiting, etc.—and develop plans for dealing with issues in each area. Remember that staff members will support what they help to create.

- **Alternative programs.** The new facility will have fewer beds than the old facility it is replacing. Based on decisions made during the system assessment and facility master planning phases, some categories of youth who were accommodated in the old facility will need to be placed in alternative programs and/or housed for shorter periods of time. A comprehensive plan should be developed for these youth, and alternative programs should be expanded and fully operational long before the move.

- **Culture change.** Serious attention must be given to creating an organizational culture that supports the values, vision, and mission that drove the design and programs for the new facility. The organizational culture is, in essence, the "personality" of an organization. In the juvenile facility, the culture may be apparent in the programs that management supports, the way things look, what staff are proud of, and how they talk to and act toward each other and the youth.

- **Post-occupancy evaluation.** Six months to a year after the new facility begins operation, the jurisdiction should evaluate the efficacy of the facility design and programs, as well as the transition process. Evaluation results form the basis of any design and programmatic changes that may be necessary.

Getting Started: Funding Considerations

Many federal and state grants are too small to pay for revamping an entire juvenile justice system or building and operating a new secure, community-based facility. These funds can, however, serve as seed money for initiating the process of changing from large institutions to smaller, community-based facilities. Such funds can also support a number of important related activities:

◆ Smaller projects ancillary to the construction of a new community-based facility.

◆ Planning studies or population analyses.

◆ Pilot programs.

◆ Development of classification instruments for use in targeting populations to be moved from large institutions to smaller, community-based facilities.

◆ Studies that help jurisdictions critically examine their classification and programming practices with an eye toward downsizing large congregate-care facilities.

Summary

Juvenile justice system and facility planning is an interactive, dynamic process of working within a community or region to (1) identify local factors that contribute to delinquency, (2) identify local strengths and resources that create resilience in youth and prevent delinquency, (3) understand the continuum of services and sanctions that address delinquency and recidivism, and (4) plan and design appropriately sized facilities that are integrated within that continuum. Underlying the process is the principle of using secure facilities only for youth who pose a threat to the community or who cannot function in a less secure setting. The ultimate goal of the process is to create a system that effectively reduces juvenile delinquency and recidivism and supports the development of healthy, productive youth.

Sample Programs

The three programs described below fit the model described in this Bulletin and are offered as a starting point for jurisdictions interested in developing facilities within that model. The author selected these samples from a list of potential model programs developed in consultation with juvenile justice system practitioners throughout the country. Many of the programs on the original list lacked a continuum of sentencing and treatment options and/or empirical evidence of effectiveness and could not, therefore, serve as samples.

Fulton Treatment Center

The Fulton Treatment Center in Missouri is a 33-bed, high-security residential treatment program for males committed to the Division of Youth Services (DYS). With funds available from a 1994 bond issue and the 1995 Juvenile Crime Bill, DYS constructed a number of smaller residential facilities (one 40-bed, four 33-bed, one 24-bed, and two 20-bed) throughout the state so that youth could receive services closer to their communities. The Fulton Treatment Center, which opened in 1997, was a prototype for these facilities.

The Fulton facility uses an open-dorm model and is enclosed and locked with a perimeter fence. Youth are placed in treatment groups of 10 to 12 participants each. They receive educational services, vocational guidance, and a variety of counseling services (group therapy, family therapy, drug and alcohol counseling, sex offender counseling, etc.). Youth who successfully complete the facility's program are released into the community and aftercare supervision with DYS.

Since fiscal year 2001, DYS has maintained a recommitment rate of 8 percent. Only 7 percent of youth discharged from DYS enter adult corrections within 5 years after their discharge.

Contact: John Klekamp
                Facility Manager
                Fulton Treatment Center
                1650 Highway O
                Fulton, MO 65251–0847
                573–592–4188
                john.klekamp@dss.mo.gov

Jackson County Youth Center

The Jackson County (Michigan) Youth Center is a secure, co-ed facility that provides infirmary/health services and an academic program, day treatment program, family services, and aftercare. The center has a total capacity of 50 beds (24 detention, 26 short-term and long-term treatment). It is part of a 5-year strategic plan that has brought improvements in the county's management of juvenile offenders, as evidenced by the following results:

◆ The day treatment program provides immediate accountability for offenders' delinquent behavior and use of illegal substances, reducing the need for detention. Of the 78 youth who participated in the program from 1999 to 2003, 40 percent successfully returned to their home schools and avoided detention; 60 percent received graduated sanctions, moving along the continuum into more restrictive settings as appropriate.

◆ The detention unit reduced its average length of stay from 21 days in 1999 to 14 days in 2002. The residential treatment program increased its rate of successful transitions from 52 percent in 1996 to 77 percent in 2001 and 65 percent in 2002.

◆ Post-treatment adjudications decreased from 20 in 1995 to 4 in 2002.

◆ From 1995 to 2002, the facility administered more than 2,500 drug screens; 16 percent of youth tested positive and received graduated sanctions and treatment as appropriate, and 84 percent tested negative and received graduated rewards for staying drug free.

Contact: Brian D. Philson
                Director
                Jackson County Youth Center
                930 Fleming Avenue
                Jackson, MI 49202
                517–788–4460
                bphilson@co.jackson.mi.us

Mendota Juvenile Treatment Center

The Mendota Juvenile Treatment Center (MJTC) in Wisconsin is a 29-bed secure correctional facility for male juveniles, located on the grounds of a state mental health institute. The mental health institute administers the MJTC program under the auspices of the state corrections department. The center uses the "decompression" treatment model to prepare the most defiant, aggressive youth for transition into conventional education, rehabilitation, and treatment settings.

The decompression model explains the behavior of the most unmanageable juvenile offenders in terms of a downward spiral in which these youth react in increasingly negative ways to deterrence-based sanctions. Sanctions beget aggression, which begets more sanctions, and so forth, until the juvenile is "compressed" into a behavior pattern of almost continual defiance. MJTC attempts to break this pattern so these youth will not withdraw (or be removed) from treatment. The MJTC program merges security with treatment when a youth's behavior becomes difficult and dangerous. If behavior requires increased security measures, individualized treatment contacts also increase. Using a "today-tomorrow" strategy, the program rates each youth daily on basic behaviors (interactions with peers and staff, following rules, etc.); acceptable behavior "today" brings more privileges "tomorrow." As youth become attached to having more privileges instead of repeating the antagonism-sanction cycle, they move toward greater involvement in school and therapy.

Regular outcome studies have compared MJTC participants with control groups to assess the effectiveness of the decompression treatment model. These studies have consistently found significant reductions in violent and felony reoffending among MJTC participants (Caldwell and Van Rybroek, 2001, in press).

Contact: Gregory J. Van Rybroek, Ph.D., J.D.
             Director
             Mendota Juvenile Treatment Center
             301 Troy Drive
             Madison, WI 53704
             608–201–1000
             VANRYGJ@dhfs.state.wi.us

Resources

Planning and Designing Juvenile Facilities

Training

Juvenile Transition and Activation Planning (J-TAP)
The curriculum for this weeklong training program is targeted to jurisdictions that are planning for the transition to and activation of new juvenile detention or correctional facilities. J-TAP is a joint project of International Partnership for Youth (IPFYouth), the National Institute of Corrections (NIC), and the Office of Juvenile Justice and Delinquency Prevention (OJJDP). For information about the program, contact Shelley Zavlek, IPFYouth, 29 Donnybrook Drive, Demarest, NJ 07627, szavlek@ipfyouth.com.

Planning of New Institutions for Juveniles (Juvenile PONI)
The curriculum for this weeklong training program is targeted to jurisdictions that are planning, designing, and building a new juvenile facility. The Juvenile PONI program helps jurisdictions make well-informed planning decisions about building new secure juvenile facilities or about renovating or expanding existing facilities. Juvenile PONI is a joint project of OJJDP and the Bureau of Justice Assistance (both within the Office of Justice Programs) and NIC. A two-page Fact Sheet on Juvenile PONI is available from OJJDP at www.ncjrs.org/pdffiles1/ojjdp/fs200101.pdf. For information on related technical assistance that NIC offers, contact Nancy Shomaker, National Institute of Corrections, 1960 Industrial Circle, Longmont, CO 80501; 800–995–6429 ext. 120; nshomaker@bop.gov.

Publications

Anticipating Space Needs in Juvenile Detention and Correctional Facilities
OJJDP Bulletin. 2001. NCJ 185234.
Available at www.ncjrs.org/pdffiles1/ojjdp/185234.pdf.

Provides juvenile justice policymakers with information to help them project detention and corrections populations. Presents an overview of the roles of juvenile justice system policies and decisionmaking in determining space needs. Analyzes methods for projecting juvenile confinement populations, noting limits of simple projection models and describing a detailed example of a comprehensive projection model. Examines practical implications of projecting detention and corrections populations and outlines differences between forecasting and predicting future space needs.

Construction, Operations, and Staff Training for Juvenile Confinement Facilities
OJJDP Juvenile Accountability Block Grants Series Bulletin. 2000. NCJ 178928.
Available at www.ncjrs.org/pdffiles1/ojjdp/178928.pdf.

Provides practical guidance on best practices with regard to juvenile confinement facilities, including information on construction decisions, master planning, facility development, operations, and staff training. Offers a step-by-step explanation of the planning process, thorough instructions on determining the type of facility needed, and a detailed discussion of the key elements of operation. Also includes extensive references and resources.

Correctional Facility Design and Detailing
American Correctional Association. Available at www.aca.org/store/bookstore.

Offers comprehensive ideas for designing, detailing, and specifying correctional facilities of all kinds, including jails, prisons, and juvenile detention facilities. Systematically examines architectural planning for state-of-the-art facilities ranging from rural settings to urban highrises. Uses modular format to combine photographs, details, specifications, and design issues. Includes case studies of new construction and remodel projects.

Planning and Design Guide for Secure Adult and Juvenile Facilities
American Correctional Association. Available at www.aca.org/store/bookstore.

Provides architects, planners, and administrators with information for designing and building facilities that are safe, secure, and architecturally sound. Shows how the elements of a correctional facility can work together. Topics include planning, design, and construction processes and issues; inmate services and programs; administrative functions; service facilities and physical plant; security features and technology; and commissioning. Also covers budget development, privatization, ADA (Americans with Disabilities Act) guidelines, outsourcing/contract services, and staffing. Contributors include top architects, planners, and administrators of adult and juvenile facilities.

Alternatives to Incarceration

Publications

Focus on Accountability: Best Practices for Juvenile Court and Probation
OJJDP Juvenile Accountability Block Grants Series Bulletin. 1999. NCJ 177611.
Available at www.ncjrs.org/pdffiles1/177611.pdf.

Describes what it means to hold juvenile offenders accountable, details the role of the juvenile court and probation department, identifies the key elements of programs that promote accountability, and presents examples of exemplary community-based initiatives. Examples include diversion, mediation and restitution, specialized probation supervision, and aftercare programs.

Juvenile Intensive Supervision: Planning Guide
OJJDP Program Summary. 1994. NCJ 150065.
Available at www.ncjrs.org/pdffiles/juvsu.pdf.

Offers practitioners tools for implementing community-based intensive supervision programs as alternatives to long-term institutional confinement for designated juvenile offenders.

Outcome Evaluation of Washington State's Research-Based Programs for Juvenile Offenders
Washington State Institute for Public Policy.
Available at www.wsipp.wa.gov/rptfiles/04-01-1201.pdf.

Documents the first statewide experiment involving research-based programs for juvenile justice, including functional family therapy, aggression replacement training, coordination of services, and multisystemic theory. Evaluates whether programs previously researched only as small-scale pilot projects work when applied statewide in a "real world" setting. Indicates that programs can be both effective and cost efficient, with savings ranging from $400 to more than $2,000 per participant.

Resources for Juvenile Detention Reform
OJJDP Fact Sheet. 2000. FS 200018.
Available at www.ncjrs.org/pdffiles1/ojjdp/fs200018.pdf.

Addresses the issue of crowding in juvenile detention facilities and describes detention reform initiatives.

Treatment Foster Care
OJJDP Family Strengthening Series Bulletin. 1998. NCJ 173421.
Available at www.ncjrs.org/pdffiles1/ojjdp/173421.pdf.

Describes an alternative to residential and group care placements for serious and chronic juvenile offenders. Includes an overview of the Treatment Foster Care approach, together with findings from evaluation studies.

Teleconference

How Shall We Respond to the Dreams of Youth?
OJJDP Teleconference. 2000. NCJ 182438.
Available online and on videotape.
See www.ojjdp.ncjrs.org/publications/PubAbstract.asp?pubi=11045.

Highlights effective interventions and model programs that serve the needs of troubled youth. Includes interviews with successful "graduates" of the juvenile justice system, footage of the system at work, and highlights from "National Juvenile Justice Summit: Revitalizing the Juvenile Court" and the National Juvenile Justice Awards.

Organizations

The organizations listed below provide guidance and information relevant to programming, planning, designing, and operating juvenile detention and correctional facilities. They also offer resources for juvenile justice system planning.

American Correctional Association. www.aca.org. 800–222–5646.

American Institute of Architects. www.aia.org. 800–242–3837.

Council for Educators of At-Risk and Delinquent Youth. www.ceardy.org. 859–622–6259.

Juvenile Justice Clearinghouse. www.ojjdp.ncjrs.org/programs/ProgSummary.asp?pi=2.
800–851–3420.

National Council of Juvenile and Family Court Judges. www.ncjfcj.org. 775–784–6012.

National Criminal Justice Reference Service. www.ncjrs.org. 800–851–3420.

National Institute of Corrections. www.nicic.org. 800–995–6429 (Academy Division). 800–877–1461 (Information Center).

National Juvenile Detention Association. www.njda.com. 859–622–6259.

National Partnership for Juvenile Services. www.npjs.org. 859–622–6259.

OJJDP National Training and Technical Assistance Center. www.nttac.org. 800–830–4031.

References

Altschuler, D.M. 1998. Intermediate sanctions and community treatment for serious and violent juvenile offenders. In *Serious and Violent Juvenile Offenders: Risk Factors and Successful Interventions*, edited by R. Loeber and D.P. Farrington. Thousand Oaks, CA: Sage Publications.

Altschuler, D.M., and Armstrong, T.L. 1994. *Intensive Aftercare for High-Risk Juveniles: An Assessment.* Washington, DC: U.S. Department of Justice, Office of Justice Programs, Office of Juvenile Justice and Delinquency Prevention.

American Correctional Association. 2001. *Directory of Adult and Juvenile Correctional Departments, Institutions, Agencies and Probation and Parole Authorities.* Lanham, MD: American Correctional Association.

Austin, J., Johnson, K.D., and Weitzer, R. Forthcoming. *Alternatives to the Secure Detention and Incarceration of Juvenile Offenders.* OJJDP Juvenile Justice Practices Series Bulletin (online only). Washington, DC: U.S. Department of Justice, Office of Justice Programs, Office of Juvenile Justice and Delinquency Prevention.

Browne, J.A. 2003. *DERAILED! The Schoolhouse to Jailhouse Track.* Washington, DC: Advancement Project.

Burke, P., Cushman, R., and Ney, B. 1996. *Guide to a Criminal Justice System Assessment.* Washington, DC: U.S. Department of Justice, National Institute of Corrections.

Burrell, S., DeMuro, P., Dunlap, E., Sanniti, C., Warboys, L. 1998. *Crowding in Juvenile Detention Centers: A Problem-Solving Manual.* Richmond, KY: National Juvenile Detention Association; Washington, DC: Youth Law Center.

Caldwell, M.F., and Van Rybroek, G.J. 2001. Efficacy of a decompression treatment model in the clinical management of violent juvenile offenders. *International Journal of Offender Therapy and Comparative Criminology* 45(4):469–477.

Caldwell, M.F., and Van Rybroek, G.J. In press. Reducing violence in serious and violent juvenile offenders using an intensive treatment program. *International Journal of Law and Mental Health.*

Catalano, R.F., Arthur, M.W., Hawkins, J.D., Berglund, L., and Olson, J.J. 1998. Comprehensive community and school-based interventions to prevent antisocial behavior. In *Serious and Violent Juvenile Offenders: Risk Factors and Successful Interventions*, edited by R. Loeber and D.P. Farrington. Thousand Oaks, CA: Sage Publications.

Center on Juvenile & Criminal Justice. 2004. Reforming the juvenile justice system. Available online at www.cjcj.org/jjic/reforming.php. Accessed November 23, 2004.

Cocozza, J.J., ed. 1992. *Responding to the Mental Health Needs of Youth in the Juvenile Justice System.* Seattle, WA: National Coalition for the Mentally Ill in the Criminal Justice System.

Coordinating Council on Juvenile Justice and Delinquency Prevention. 1996. *Combating Violence and Delinquency: The National Juvenile Justice Action Plan.* Summary. Washington, DC: U.S. Department of Justice, Office of Justice Programs, Office of Juvenile Justice and Delinquency Prevention.

Farrington, D.P. 1996. The explanation and prevention of youthful offending. In *Delinquency and Crime: Current Theories,* edited by J.D. Hawkins. Cambridge, UK: Cambridge University Press.

Feld, B.C. 1998. Juvenile and criminal justice systems' responses to youth violence. In *Youth Violence: Crime and Justice: A Review of Research,* Vol. 24, edited by M. Tonry and M.H. Moore. Chicago, IL: University of Chicago Press.

Griffinger, W. 2001. National trends, local consequences: The expansion of juvenile detention facilities. *Youth Law News* XXII(1):18–21.

Hawkins, J.D., Catalano, R.F., and Miller, J.Y. 1992. Risk and protective factors for alcohol and other drug problems in adolescence and early adulthood: Implications for drug abuse prevention. *Psychological Bulletin* 112:64–105.

Hawkins, J.D., Herrenkohl, T.I., Farrington, D.P., Brewer, D., Catalano, R.F., Harachi, T.W., and Cothern, L. 2000. *Predictors of Youth Violence.* Washington, DC: U.S. Department of Justice, Office of Justice Programs, Office of Juvenile Justice and Delinquency Prevention.

Hobbs, F., and Nicole, S. 2002. *Demographic Trends in the 20th Century, U.S. Census Bureau, Census 2000 Special Reports, Series CENSR-4.* Washington, DC: U.S. Government Printing Office.

Howell, J.C., ed. 1995. *Guide for Implementing the Comprehensive Strategy for Serious, Violent, and Chronic Juvenile Offenders.* Washington, DC: U.S. Department of Justice, Office of Justice Programs, Office of Juvenile Justice and Delinquency Prevention.

Howell, J.C. 1997. *Juvenile Justice and Youth Violence.* Thousand Oaks, CA: Sage Publications.
Hsia, H.H., and Beyer, M. 2000. *System Change Through State Challenge Activities: Approaches and Products.* Bulletin. Washington, DC: U.S. Department of Justice, Office of Justice Programs, Office of Juvenile Justice and Delinquency Prevention.

Krisberg, B., and Howell, J.C. 1998. The impact of the juvenile justice system and prospects for graduated sanctions in a comprehensive strategy. In *Serious and Violent Juvenile Offenders: Risk Factors and Successful Interventions,* edited by R. Loeber and D.P. Farrington. Thousand Oaks, CA: Sage Publications.

Krisberg, B., Onek, D., Jones, M., and Schwartz, I. 1993. *Juveniles in State Custody: Prospects for Community-Based Care of Troubled Adolescents.* San Francisco, CA: National Council on Crime and Delinquency.

Langan, P.A., and Levin, D.J. 2002. *Recidivism of Prisoners Released in 1994.* Washington, D.C. U.S. Department of Justice, Office of Justice Programs, Bureau of Justice Statistics.

Lipsey, M.W., and Wilson, D.B. 1998. Effective intervention for serious juvenile offenders: A synthesis of research. In *Serious and Violent Juvenile Offenders: Risk Factors and Successful Interventions,* edited by R. Loeber and D.P. Farrington. Thousand Oaks, CA: Sage Publications.

Loeber, R., and Farrington, D.P., eds. 1998. *Serious and Violent Juvenile Offenders: Risk Factors and Successful Interventions.* Thousand Oaks, CA, Sage Publications, pp. 313–345.

Masten, A.S., and Coatsworth, J.D. 1998. The development of competence in favorable and unfavorable environments: A tale of resources, risk and resilience. *American Psychologist* 53:205–220.

McCord, J., Widom, C.S., and Crowell, N.A., eds. 2001. *Juvenile Crime, Juvenile Justice.* Washington, DC: National Academy Press.

Mendel, R.A. 2000. *Less Hype, More Help: Reducing Juvenile Crime, What Works—and What Doesn't.* Washington, DC: American Youth Policy Forum.

Mendel, R.A. 2001. *Less Cost, More Safety: Guiding Lights for Reform in Juvenile Justice.* Washington, DC: American Youth Policy Forum.

Parent, D., Leiter, V., Kennedy, S., Livens, L., Wentworth, D., and Wilcox, S. 1994. *Conditions of Confinement: Juvenile Detention and Corrections Facilities.* Research Report. Washington, DC: U.S. Department of Justice, Office of Justice Programs, Office of Juvenile Justice and Delinquency Prevention.

Puritz, P., and Scali, M. 1998. *Beyond the Walls: Improving the Conditions of Confinement for Youth in Custody.* Report. Washington, DC: U.S. Department of Justice, Office of Justice Programs, Office of Juvenile Justice and Delinquency Prevention.

Roush, D., and McMillen, M. 2000. *Construction, Operations, and Staff Training for Juvenile Confinement Facilities.* Juvenile Accountability Block Grants Series Bulletin. Washington, DC: U.S. Department of Justice, Office of Justice Programs, Office of Juvenile Justice and Delinquency Prevention.

Sickmund, M. 2002. *Juvenile Offenders in Residential Placement: 1997–1999.* Fact Sheet. Washington, DC: U.S. Department of Justice, Office of Justice Programs, Office of Juvenile Justice and Delinquency Prevention.

Sickmund, M., Sladky, T.J., and Kang, W. 2004. Census of juveniles in residential placement databook. Available online at www.ojjdp.ncjrs.org/ojstatbb/cjrp. Accessed November 23, 2004.

Snyder, H.N. 2003. *Juvenile Arrests 2001.* Bulletin. Washington, DC: U.S. Department of Justice, Office of Justice Programs, Office of Juvenile Justice and Delinquency Prevention.

Snyder, H.N. 2004. *Juvenile Arrests 2002.* Bulletin. Washington, DC: U.S. Department of Justice, Office of Justice Programs, Office of Juvenile Justice and Delinquency Prevention.

Snyder, H.N., and Sickmund, M. 1999. *Juvenile Offenders and Victims: 1999 National Report.* Washington, DC: U.S. Department of Justice, Office of Justice Programs, Office of Juvenile Justice and Delinquency Prevention.

Stanfield, R. 1999. *Pathways to Juvenile Detention Reform: The JDAI Story.* Baltimore, MD: The Annie E. Casey Foundation.

Teplin, L., Abram, K., McClelland, G., Dulcan, M., Mericle, A. 2002. Psychiatric disorders in youth in juvenile detention. *Archives of General Psychiatry* 59(12):1133–1143.

Thornberry, T.P. 1993. *The Relationship Between Childhood Maltreatment and Adolescent Involvement in Delinquency and Drug Use.* Albany, NY: State University of New York at Albany.

Torbet, P., Gable, R., Hurst, H. IV, Montgomery, I., Szymanski, L., Thomas, D. 1996. *State Responses to Serious and Violent Juvenile Crime.* Report. Washington, DC: U.S. Department of Justice, Office of Justice Programs, Office of Juvenile Justice and Delinquency Prevention.

Torbet, P., and Szymanski, L. 1998. *State Legislative Responses to Violent Crime: 1996–97 Update.* Bulletin. Washington, DC: U.S. Department of Justice, Office of Justice Programs, Office of Juvenile Justice and Delinquency Prevention.

Wiebush, R., Baird, C., Krisberg, B., and Onek, D. 1995. Risk assessment and classification for serious, violent, and chronic offenders. In *Serious and Violent Juvenile Offenders: Risk Factors and Successful Interventions,* edited by R. Loeber and D.P. Farrington. Thousand Oaks, CA: Sage Publications.

Wilson, J., and Howell, J.C. 1993. *The Comprehensive Strategy for Serious, Violent, and Chronic Juvenile Offenders.* Washington, DC: U.S. Department of Justice, Office of Justice Programs, Office of Juvenile Justice and Delinquency Prevention.

Zavlek, S., and Barron, D. 2000. Teamwork: National workshop addresses planning strategies for the juvenile justice system. *Corrections Today* 62 (December).

Acknowledgments

This Bulletin was written by Shelley Zavlek, M.Ed., J.D., President of International Partnership for Youth/Justice Solutions Group. Ms. Zavlek, formerly Executive Director of Capital and Operational Planning for the New York City Department of Juvenile Justice, has more than 25 years of experience in justice system and facility administration and planning, law, and education. Under cooperative agreements with the National Institute of Corrections (NIC) and supported by funding from OJJDP, Ms. Zavlek has developed two weeklong courses addressing the challenges of planning for and opening new juvenile detention and correctional facilities. She has presented these programs—Planning of New Institutions for Juvenile Facilities (Juvenile PONI) and Juvenile Transition and Activation Planning (J–TAP)—to numerous jurisdictions across the country. She currently provides technical assistance on planning, designing, and operating juvenile and adult correctional facilities to 22 American Indian and Alaska Native tribes under a cooperative agreement with NIC. As part of this cooperative agreement, Ms. Zavlek has overseen the development of a series of guides on planning, designing, and constructing detention and correctional facilities in Indian Country.

Ms. Zavlek is a member of the Governing Board of the National Partnership for Juvenile Services, President and a founding member of the Council for Educators of At-Risk and Delinquent Youth, and a member of the Juvenile Corrections Committee of the American Correctional Association.

Ms. Zavlek is grateful for the valuable editorial assistance and input of Mark Martin and Anthony Jones during the development of this Bulletin.

This Bulletin was prepared under contract number OJP–2000–298–BF from the Office of Juvenile Justice and Delinquency Prevention.

The Office of Juvenile Justice and Delinquency Prevention is a component of the Office of Justice Programs, which also includes the Bureau of Justice Assistance, the Bureau of Justice Statistics, the National Institute of Justice, and the Office for Victims of Crime.

NCJ 209326